Decodable

My Cap

Written by Sue Bear
Illustrated by Lori Burk

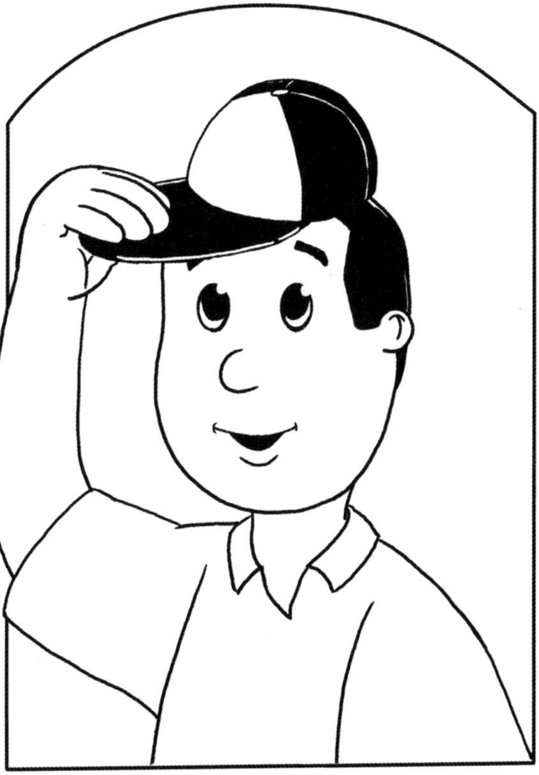

Phonics Skill

Consonant Cc /k/

Cam Mac cap

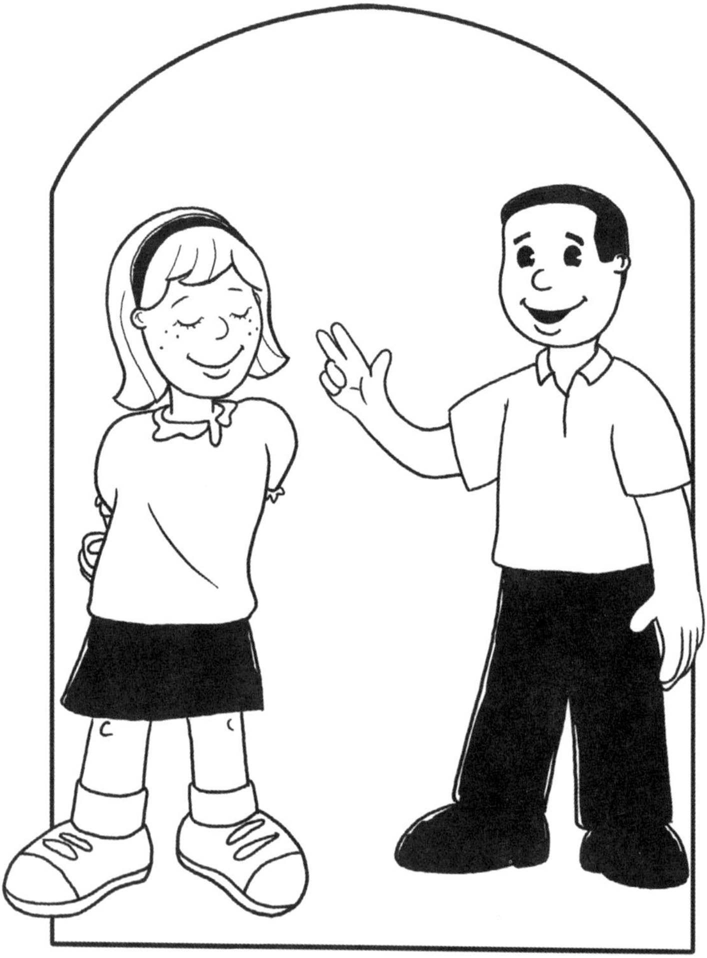

I am Cam.
I am Mac.

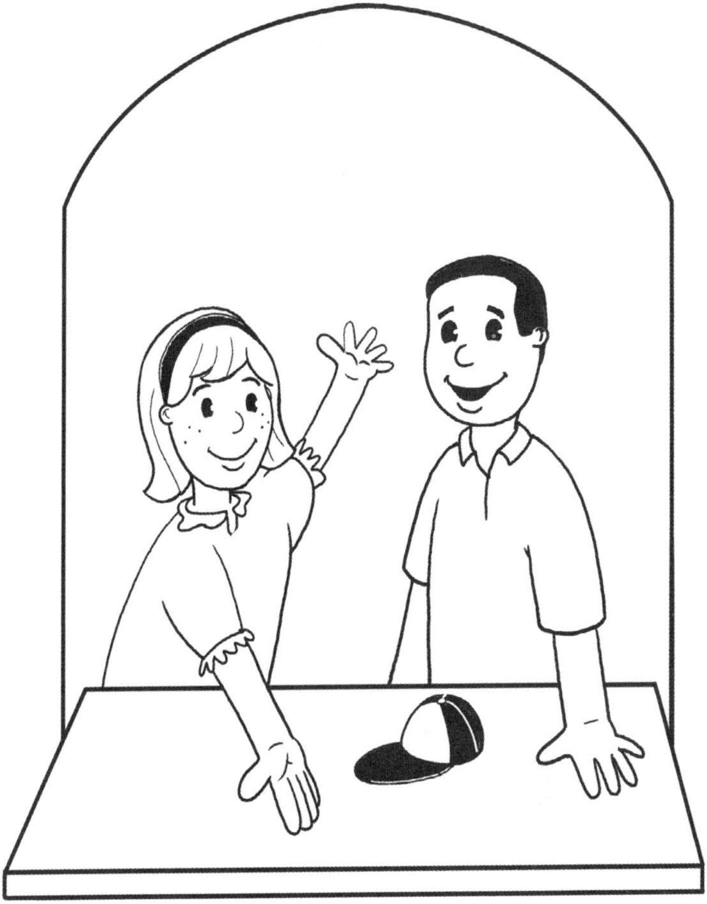

We have a cap.

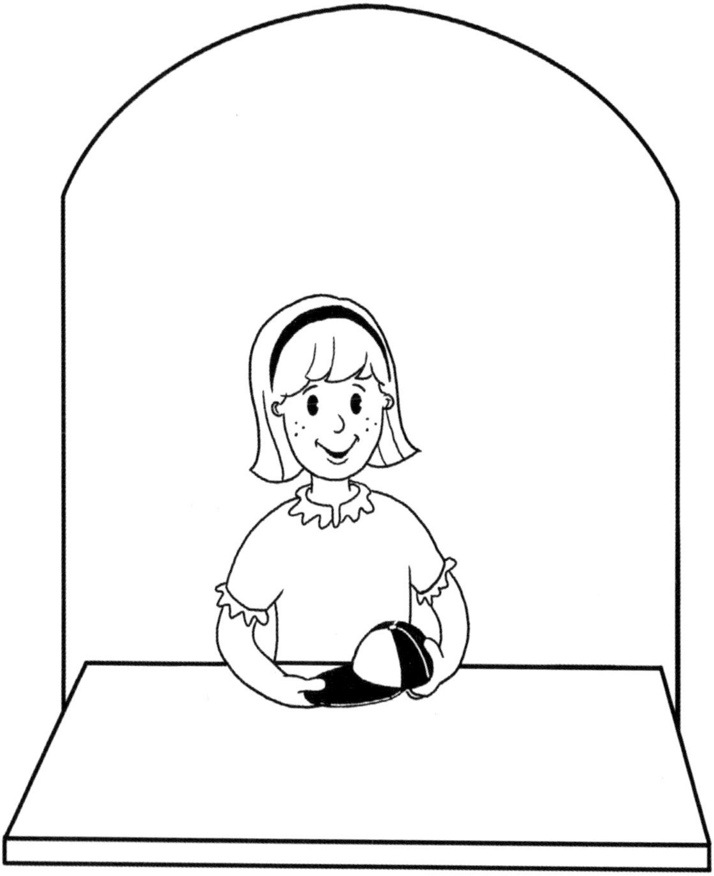

Cam is at the cap.

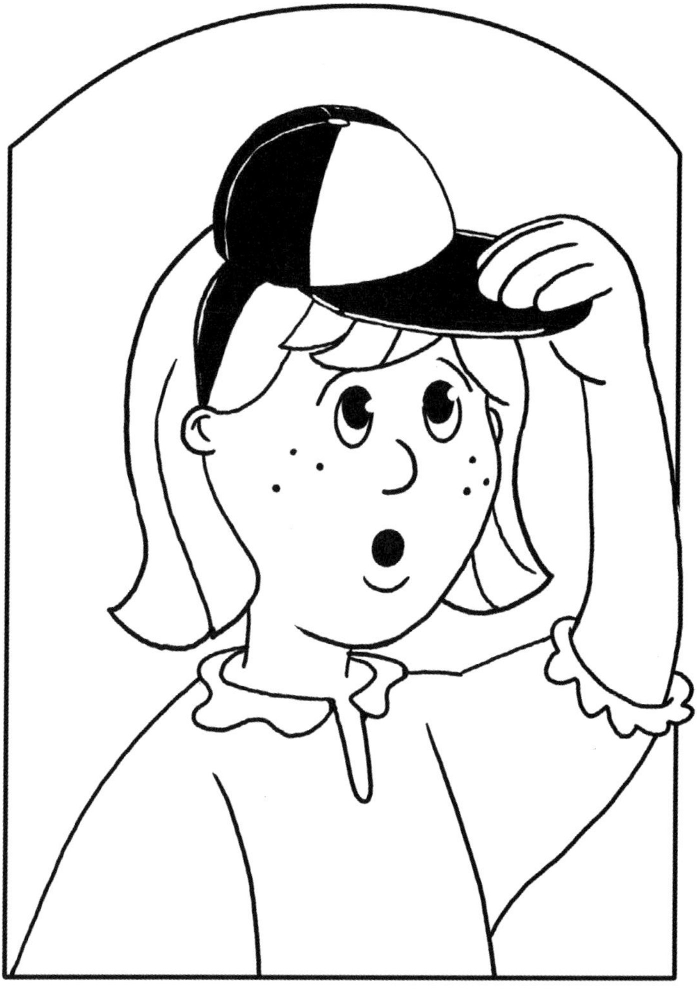

Is the cap my cap?

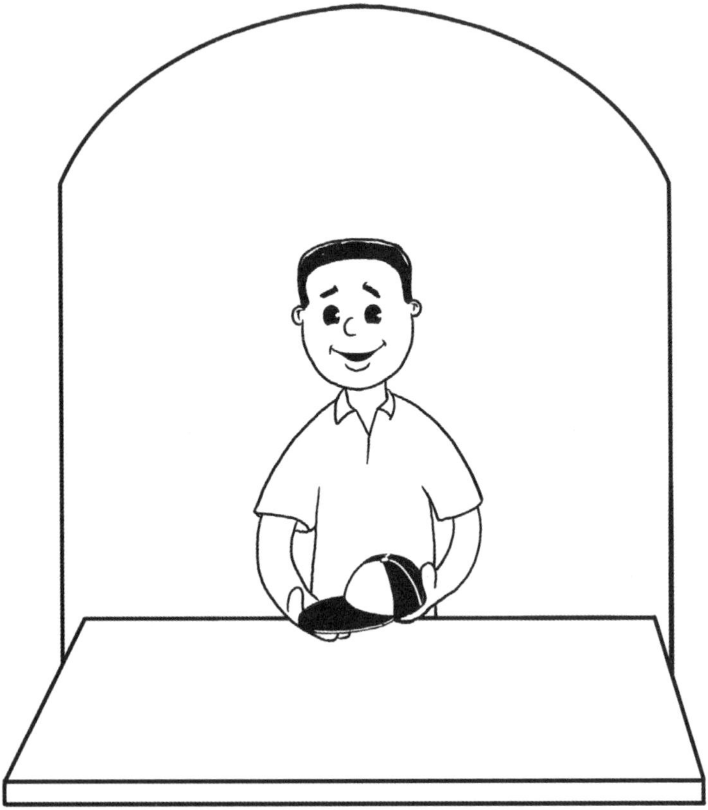

Mac is at the cap.

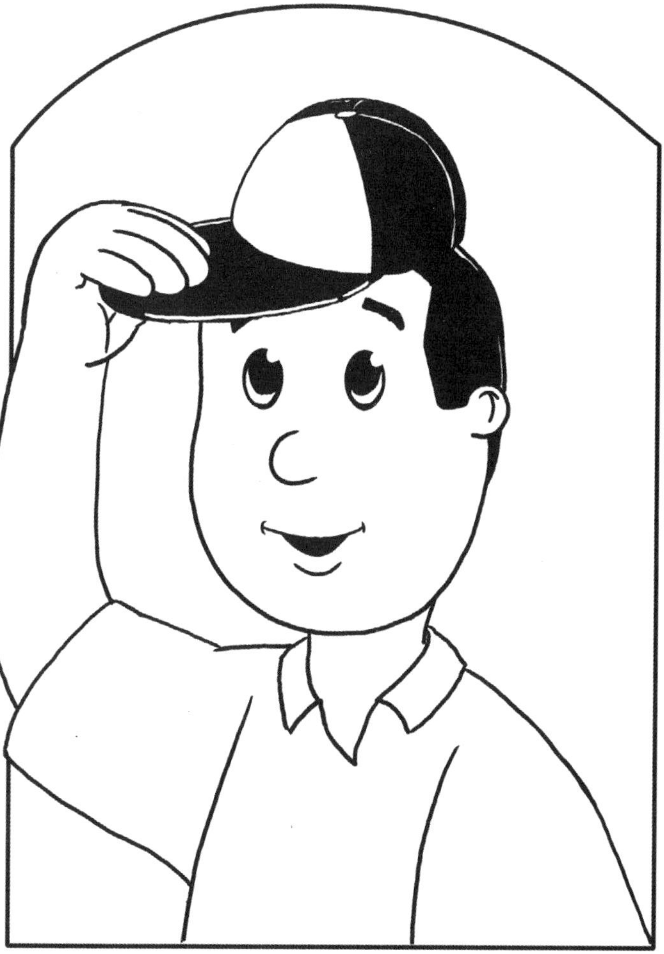

Is the cap my cap?

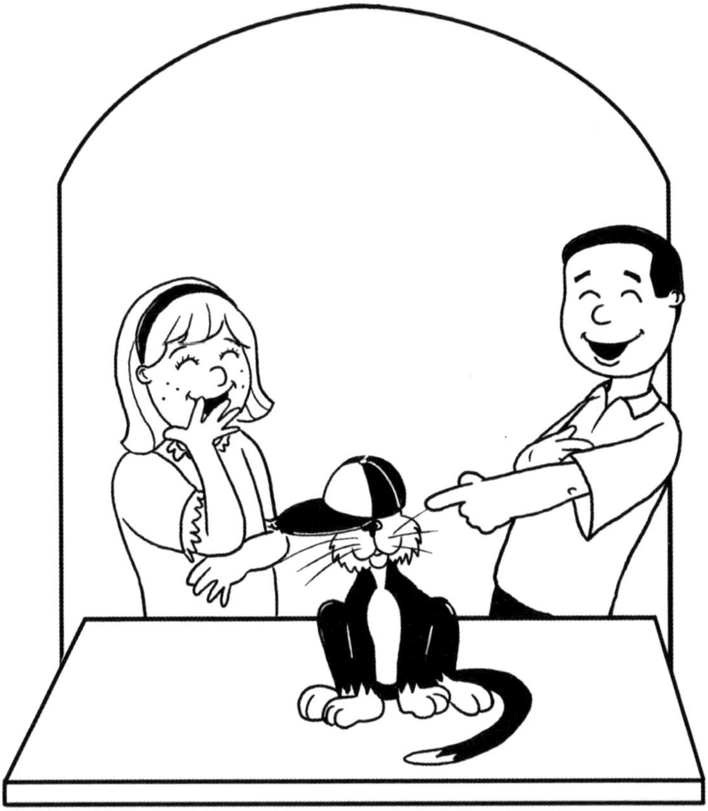

I like my cap.